TRANSGENDER AMERICA

Spirit, Identity, And The Emergence Of The Third Gender

TRANSGENDER AMERICA

Spirit, Identity, And The Emergence Of The Third Gender

S. F. Howe

Diamond Star Press
Los Angeles

Author Website: http://SFHowe.com

Transgender America: Spirit, Identity, And The Emergence Of The Third Gender

Copyright © 2018 S. F. Howe
Published by Diamond Star Press

First Edition
ISBN 13: 9780977433520
ISBN 10: 0977433528

Books by S. F. Howe

Matrix Man
How To Become Enlightened, Happy And Free In An
Illusion World

The Top Ten Myths Of Enlightenment
Exposing The Truth About Spiritual Enlightenment
That Will Set You Free!

The Bringer
How To Free Yourself From The Mind Control
Programs Of The Matrix Reality
Coming Soon!

Secrets Of The Plant Whisperer
How To Care For, Connect, And
Communicate With Your House Plants

Your Plant Speaks!
How To Use Your Houseplant As A Therapist
Coming Soon!

Vision Board Success
How To Get Everything You Want With Vision
Boards!

Sex Yoga
The 7 Easy Steps To A Mind-Blowing Kundalini
Awakening!

Transgender America
Spirit, Identity, And The Emergence
Of The Third Gender

Morning Routine For Night Owls
How To Supercharge Your Day With A Gentle Yet
Powerful Morning Routine!

When Nothing Else Works
How To Cure Your Lower Back Pain Fast!

Free Gift

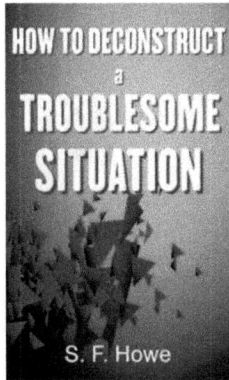

As my thanks to you for reading *Transgender America: Spirit, Identity, And The Emergence Of The Third Gender,* I would like you to have the bonus report, "How to Deconstruct a Troublesome Situation." Inside this report is a powerful technique that will help you strip any problem down to its core and give you the objectivity needed to find the best solution.

To download your free gift, just go to https://bit.ly/DeconstructSituation.

For all people who are struggling with gender identity issues or have a loved one who is; that you may find peace, healing and freedom.

Table of Contents

Setting the Ground Rules

L et me begin by saying what this book is *not*: it is not intended to judge, change, fix or improve anything about your gender assignment or your sexual orientation. Nor is it intended as a discussion or debate about sexual orientation, homosexuality or other sexual preferences.

Additionally, we also need to understand that gender is not the same thing as sexual orientation. Those two subjects are often mistaken for one another, so let us make the distinction that gender refers to biological status, e.g., male or female, and that sexual orientation refers to sexual practices and preferences.

What this book *is* about is gender, gender identity and gender dysphoria. For the clarity of this discussion, let us agree that gender refers to your sex assignment at birth, usually male or female. Let us further agree that gender identity issues and gender dysphoria refer to your attitudes and reactions to your gender assignment at birth, and to gender in general, as well as to the social behaviors and roles expected of members of your sex.

The purpose of this book is to provide a spiritual, social and political perspective on the burgeoning transgender and gender identity movement. My intent is to support you in making more objective inferences, determinations and decisions for your own life, rather than being swept away on a cultural tsunami.

Introduction

Welcome to the Transgender Agenda

Many people who are conflicted about their gender identity, uncomfortable with their gender or sexual expression in our culture, or who are hiding their sexual orientation eventually 'come out' and take a stand. To that end, there are any number of groups, organizations and public events that help support and solidify one's identification with an alternative orientation.

For someone who has been suffering in private about their sexuality or gender identity, finding support can be an important step toward self-acceptance. However, there is little to no attention or support for seeking awareness of the higher truth about gender and the body, not to mention about life on earth in general; a higher awareness that might alter your perspective and, therefore, your reactions and your choices. This book aims, in some small measure, to bridge that gap.

Also little known is the fact that the fast-growing cultural obsession with gender identity, which has been glibly attributed to millenials, has actually been socially engineered behind the scenes and is being aggressively rolled out as we speak. This operation, otherwise known as the Transgender Agenda, raises many questions which will be addressed later in this book.

When you understand, as we shall explain, that the body is an illusion and that illusions do not desire, cannot create and do not have an independent existence, you will recognize that it is your mind creating gender and sexual orientation issues, not your body. A mind can be influenced, overridden and hypnotized to accept

almost anything if that programming is performed over time with consistency, frequency
and power.

Once this is understood, any force, belief, im-
pression or input that encourages your mind to
view your body as a creative entity, and thereby
causes you to become obsessed with your biolo-
gy or sexuality, including redefining your sexuality or your gender, coming out as this or that, or
actually surgically changing your gender, is
something that is taking you away from the truth
of who you really are. It does this by grinding
you deeper into the physical as if the physical
were all there is when the physical is only the
surface level of this illusion world.

Understanding the bigger picture of life on
earth enables you to put your gender and sexuality issues in perspective. For those open to these
words, it will save you from a lifetime of focusing on the wrong thing—your sexuality or your
gender identity—rather than the right thing—
your true, infinite spiritual identity which is
genderless. There is no gender in Spirit; gender

only exists in this illusion world and all other physical illusion realms.

You come here into this earth realm to have a certain experience, to play the role of a certain persona. Why do you do this? Because the Infinite Being who you really are expresses itself infinitely in form. It creates the form, it materializes the form with the substance of its own Being and it sustains the form.

Whether straight or gay, gender content or gender-conflicted, this book will gently guide you through the mental and emotional steps you need to take to shed your obsession with your physical body, your gender and your sexual identity. It will ultimately help free you from the pernicious 'identification with body' syndrome (otherwise known as body ID) which renders those who are body ID'd in a lowered state of consciousness rooted in ignorance of truth. A sustained lowering of consciousness results in a breach with Source. This allows the controllers of our culture, meaning the overseers of the system, the establishment and the institutions, to substitute their agenda and to move you in the direction that suits their needs.

But please note that not only are those struggling with gender identity or sexual orientation vulnerable to the consciousness trap of body ID; so also are the vast majority of the straight population. Body ID or the absence thereof is one of the defining factors for spiritual awareness. The less you are identified with body, the higher your being vibrates and, as a result, the more spiritual truth becomes available to you. Conversely, the more spiritually advanced you are, the faster your being vibrates, the more spiritual truth is available to you, and the less you are identified with your body. In your highest state, you are One with Source and have access to Infinite Truth.

Body ID is one of the key experiential traps that causes you to remain locked into your programming in our matrix-like illusion world. Hence, real freedom is not about obsessing about or taking action on your gender or sexual identity issues but about recognizing your true identity as an Infinite Being.

This book will guide you step by step into an understanding of your true self as the Infinite and will enable you to put your culturally induced sex and gender obsession in its rightful place. This shift in perspective, once made, will bring the peace and freedom you have longed for but may have never known before.

In the following chapter, we will begin to chip away at the false structure maintaining body ID by briefly reviewing the history of gender identity and exploring how spiritual Wholeness relates to gender.

Chapter 1

Wholeness vs. Gender

We have been locked into gender roles throughout all of our centuries of existence on this planet. Reproduction and survival of the species naturally created a division of labor and the resulting expected behavior for men and women. In indigenous populations, men typically hunted large game and provided protection for the tribe while women raised the children, maintained the hearth fires, and gathered berries, grubs and other small foodstuffs.

However, even primitive cultures allowed an alternative path for the few who could not fit into the traditional roles. Those individuals often demonstrated special gifts, such as psychic or healing abilities. For example, if a man had the ability to see visions or tell the future and refused to participate in the typical male activities, he would dress like a woman and become the resident shaman. The shaman performed healings, predicted future events, and led the tribe in their fertility, hunting or warrior rituals. Similarly, if a female felt unsuited to her traditional role or was unable to bear children she might serve as a medicine woman or visionary for the tribe.

In the modern world, the expected behavior of men and women has been variously outlined by our institutions rather than by our primal nature. These institutions include but are not limited to the State, religion, the military, the media, the entertainment industry, the educational establishment, and the medical establishment. Gender expectations are further reinforced and maintained by the family such that, to this day, the family is the primary enforcer of the system and of the demands of the various institutions of our culture.

While recognizing that there are degrees of gender identity expression across a bell curve of human behavior, the generally accepted range of behavior for males and females in our culture has historically been quite rigid. Men are the providers, the leaders and warriors, women the obedient housekeepers and breeders.

In more recent times some women have sought freedom from the bondage of their gender roles to express more of their total self through education, employment and creative self-expression. Similarly, some men have sought freedom from the burden of their responsibilities as provider, leader and fighter in order to express more of their creative and nurturing side.

Western society allows these variations within the overall bell curve of acceptable behavior, but the price one pays can be increasingly steep the further from the center you move.

Seeking fulfillment, women who attempt to have both families and careers may find themselves on a treadmill of activity that never stops long enough to give them a moment's peace. Because of the nature of the system, their work within the system is likely to be not nearly as fulfilling as they may have once dreamt it would be and becomes more about the paycheck than true expression.

Men who stay home with the kids or withdraw from competitive arenas to express unique talents may find themselves struggling to contribute financially and living in fear of being judged by others as weak or effeminate.

Even worse is that most people have absorbed so many false beliefs about their true nature, about life, about the world, about who they should be and what they should do, not to mention about who *you* should be and what *you* should do, that when the truth of Wholeness is revealed they experience 'truth shock' which triggers the immediate denial of what they are hearing and the inevitable name-calling of the messenger.

The spiritual truth of your Infinite Being as Wholeness in an illusion world could seem insane to someone heavily programmed by the State, which is the vast majority. After all, how does it fit with the idea of a white-bearded God in the sky who is like a moody king that has to be worshipped and pleased? Much less does it explain the obviously real and solid three-dimensional world containing many dangers, within which you are born, live for a short time and die.

So what exactly is this spiritual truth we are referring to? Let us begin by exploring the concept of Wholeness and how it relates to and ultimately overshadows the physical illusion of gender.

Spiritual Wholeness is an attribute of your Infinite Self or Infinite Being. It goes to the core of your existence by recognizing that this corporeal body you inhabit is like a shadow puppet of the real you which is invisible. That real you is Infinite, Perfect and Whole. Furthermore, it is the same Infinite Being of everyone and everything.

What, you ask, everyone is the same Being? Exactly. Not only is everyone lived by the same Being, but that Being is the substance of all form, including the very air you breathe. There is nothing that isn't Infinite Being and nowhere you can go where Infinite Being is not. You live, breathe, and move within the Infinite like a fish swimming in the ocean or a bird taking flight in the sky.

Wholeness is just another term for Infinite Self or Infinite Being. It describes the aspect of the Infinite that represents perfect order, harmony and health. When the body is brought under the aegis of Wholeness, there can be nothing but Divine Order, Divine Harmony and Divine Health.

From the perspective of Wholeness, any perception of bodily imperfection or any dissatisfaction with one's gender assignment is shown as what it is—a mental creation and preoccupation, not a spiritual truth.

In this world, there is the body, the mind and the spirit. Spiritual truth is always the one and only truth. It remains locked away in its tower of perfection until we raise our consciousness out of the hypnosis of the human scene, with all of its conflicting ideologies, and align with It. When a deep and sustained connection is made with our true identity as Infinite Spirit, harmony unfolds in our experience and peace and joy fill our hearts.

Unfortunately, most of us are consumed with the physical world and all of its struggles and delights. The invisible spiritual realm may not have any meaning to us whatsoever, or may be easily displaced in the press of everyday life.

Life brings us 'down to earth' on a regular basis. Our minds have been heavily programmed by our culture to see this world as all there is. We are programmed to see our bodies as independent, creative entities that have the ability to be born, grow up, grow old and die, while along the way they might 'get sick,' suffer identity issues or, in some cases, cry out for gender reassignment.

Once we fully understand the truth about this reality, it becomes our responsibility to do all we can to raise ourselves up and sustain ourselves in the higher truth of Spiritual Wholeness. In so doing, we transform our perception of our body and bring peace and healing to our souls.

In the next chapter we will delve into the nature of Body and explore the body's true spiritual place in our lives. Once we have grasped the meaning and purpose of our bodies, we will have taken a big first step toward making peace with body-related issues.

When you take all the steps outlined in the following chapters, by the time you reach the end of this book you will be well on your way towards freedom from the pain of gender identity issues as well as from gender assignment and other body concerns.

Chapter 2

The Truth About Your Body

Everyone would agree that their body is a separate, independent entity; after all, your body stands alone and no one but you can inhabit your body, feel what it feels or do what it does. But what if I were to tell you that your body is the surface manifestation of a multidimensional being and that this Infinite Being is the substance of all bodies, that, in fact, there is only one Body and all seemingly separate bodies are projections of the One Body?

Follow along on this line of thinking, dear reader, and you may find yourself feeling increased freedom from your programming by the end of this chapter.

As mentioned, your physical body is a replica of the One Body, but with customizations to suit its purposes in being your unique surface representation. Yes, this world you find yourself in is the Surface World, and all that exists here, even the inanimate objects, have a multidimensional existence in other worlds.

Like an echo traveling through the corridors of time and space, all vibrational entities which appear as matter in your world, exist in infinite worlds where they appear according to their purpose in that world. Some worlds are very similar to this one and others completely disparate. There is a plan for every purpose and a purpose for every place.

You are a being of this world, the planet Earth. Your body is the surface manifestation of your multidimensional spirit which exists throughout all of eternity. There are no divisions in the bigger picture, dear reader. Everything is One, for, in truth, The All That Is, the Absolute, is the substance of all form no matter your locus in space or time.

Your ultimate identity is the All, which is the truth of who you really are. And what is your body but a surface representation of the All for your story in this reality.

We begin this chapter with the biggest picture because it provides a foundation for all else that you shall learn; everything is ultimately One, which is the Consciousness of All.

So what does it mean to have a body in your reality? A body is a spiritual entity as are all things. A body is a spiritual symbol of the Great You as it traverses this minute corner of Infinity.

You cannot understand body without contemplating infinity even where they appear to be opposite. The body is finite, is it not? Yet infinity is, well, infinite. Dear reader, these divisions are false as all things are infinite, immortal life. You body dies to this plane, yes, but the real you is born onto another plane in another 'body' that represents you there.

What is this 'you' we are talking about? It is one of innumerable representations of the All in the unlimited realms of existence, which is having experiences and gathering data for the never-ending knowledgebase of Being in Form. Without form, The All exists as Great Potential or Nothingness. That isn't meant to denigrate it, but to describe the Unmanifest All as Being without purpose.

When Being conceived of becoming form and experiencing consciousness from within the limitations of existence, it found its purpose. You, a sojourner of the realms, feed data back to your Higher Self, which in turn informs a hierarchy of beings, which are themselves just variations of the One, the ultimate repository of all knowledge.

The One holds all that is in a field of objective consciousness. This is the true meaning of divine love. Objective consciousness has no attachments, no conditioning and no prior agenda. It is love because it does not seek to change its creations or judge them. It holds all that is in a field of love.

This field is so far removed from human love, with its changing affections, emotional demands, needs, indulgences and expectations, as to be unrecognizable. Human love is merely an artifact of the love of the One and has no real likeness.

The One loves you through your body and through the forms within the realm you inhabit. The One is the substance of all form including the very air you breathe. There is nowhere the One is not. We tell you this to make clear the true derivation of Body — both the One Body and all seemingly separate bodies. They are an integral and inseparable part of the One. They are made as an illusion of physical for this biologically designed realm called earth.

Some realms have light or sound as their primary reference point, while other realms have various degrees of biological design, as does yours. Please note, however, it is a design, not an immutable reality, much like a stage set is for movie scenes shot in a studio. Some sets appear to be the inside of homes while others resemble an outdoor scene. But when you pull back from the set, you see the engineers moving set pieces and the designers making small touches to the scenery. Such is the truth of a biological world. It appears completely real, but it is a design for a purpose.

Now on to the human body which is often labeled the most advanced biological creation in this world. I hope you can see that the body appears to be biological to the core, but is really a set piece as it were. It is tweaked by your Higher Self prior to running your story so that it correctly represents you, but is no more real than stage sets in a movie. It is a representation of you down to the tiniest detail, however, and for that reason is as important a creation as if it were truly physical.

In the following chapter, we will continue our spiritual exploration of the meaning of Body and why the body does not create anything, including illness or gender dysphoria. At the end of that chapter, we provide a simple technique to help you heal your own physical, mental or emotional issues around body and/or gender identity.

Chapter 3

The Body Does Not Create

There is nothing physical within the Consciousness of the All, as the All is a nonphysical being that creates the illusion of matter from non-physical manifestations of its own consciousness. Therefore, you may now know that your body is an illusion of matter.

This knowledge is the key to self healing in your reality because it underlines the mutable and ephemeral nature of body. With this understanding firmly grasped you may proceed to heal or more accurately discreate any illusion ailment or body-related issue that is now appearing.

Healing presupposes the presence of an injury, disease or other issue that needs to be fixed, treated or eradicated, whereas to 'discreate' means to erase a miscreation appearing as real.

Your concerns about gender, gender assignment and/or gender identity are hypnotically induced miscreations appearing as real. This is not to say that you are at fault for having these concerns. All that it means is that you have picked up subconsciously, from the collective consciousness, a disturbance about your gender.

This gender disturbance is, as are all mental, emotional and/or physical ailments, mesmeric suggestion from the outer and inner worlds of your realm. It may have its seemingly logical source in private internal feelings about yourself, perhaps dating back to earliest childhood, or in your frustrations with cultural limitations imposed on free expression of identity. However, your gender identity issue is also part of an actual 'deep state' campaign to disconnect you from your spiritual source by focusing you on the body and, specifically, its gender and sexual expression.

A being on this planet disconnected from their spiritual source is a being that exists in a lowered vibration. What is a lowered vibration but a lesser state with filters that automatically block access to your highest potential, in this case filters that focus you on body and gender issues. A lowered vibration changes everything about a person, and more importantly causes them to believe their mind chatter with its negative, fearful thoughts.

In reading this, you may object vehemently at this point. You likely feel it all-important to focus on your identity issue and perhaps to demonstrate as an activist in support of your cause, or to otherwise signal to the world your uniqueness and freedom from gender stereotypes.

Furthermore, you may urgently want to register your objection to the rigid cultural programs and to the bullying and humiliation you may fear or have actually suffered when your individuality was rejected or made fun of by others. You probably are convinced that it is critically important that the world be made to stretch its belief system to embrace pan-identity as you have.

In truth, the world is what it is, and that includes its multi-layers of conflicting ideology. Not only is true freedom discouraged at every turn and deeply contradicted by the teachings and practices of all the cultural institutions, but also even your gender identity issue, and everything you do and feel that is associated with it, has been both scripted and co-opted by the State in service of a nefarious purpose which we will discuss in a later chapter.

So how are miscreations discreated? First of all, they are not banished from the same level of consciousness that created them. Miscreations are subconscious energy patterns that have taken form in the mind and have a symbolic meaning to the consciousness of that individual. These energy patterns give rise to forms that seem very physical and real, but have in truth all the substance of a dream, meaning they have no permanent or lasting value. It is the vibration of Earth that attributes fixed and hard reality to these wisps of smoke.

The person suffering from an ailment of body or soul is no different from someone hypnotized by a stage hypnotist to be temporarily paralyzed or to perform feats they would be incapable of in their ordinary consciousness. But 'real life' is not a stage show and the culture takes a literal view of whatever appears in physical reality. Ailments are treated as being entirely real and imbued with deadly importance. If it is a physical ill, various techniques, medicines, contraptions and surgeries, conventional or alternative, may be offered or sought out, all of which shout the reality of the ailment. As a matter of course, doctors will cite the worst case scenario for your condition to scare you into submission.

In knowing that the whole of reality and, in particular, the ailments of earth are nothing but mesmerism is to know the truth. However, knowing this intellectually does not necessarily dispatch an illusion. So much belief is invested in the physical illusion it is not realistic to assume that you can discreate a dire diagnosis through talking yourself out of it. All the while the problem stares you in the face, perhaps overwhelms you with pain and fear.

The mesmerism in fact preceded the appearance of the 'illness,' so by the time it manifested, the underlying process was fully in place. To fight illusions that you are secretly or subconsciously convinced are fact is a losing battle.

The best path for handling the unwanted appearance of an illness, or of a mental or emotional disturbance, is to first recognize that now that it has made its appearance, there is no value in wasting your time denying its apparent reality. The mesmerism has already been established.

Wisdom dictates adopting an attitude of unconcern. This attitude combines a comprehension of the greater truth of reality and of how ailments and issues come into being with a release of the emotional demand to be relieved of it.

Instead of trying to convince yourself that what is appearing is not real or trying to figure out how to fix it, your job is to raise the vibration of your reaction to the issue. Even if the initial situation triggered fear and pain, the approach is always to raise the vibration of your reaction to it. This need not be rushed, and is often impossible to rush, as a process occurs with the initial onset.

The greatest anxiety and discomfort is invariably at the onset. Don't expect to be peaceful and happy if you are embattled by fear and discomfort while in the throes of the first onset of your issue or illness. Do whatever you can to relieve your discomfort but understand it is normal to feel that way. To come into acceptance of your new condition begins with accepting how you feel right now and not denigrating yourself for it or expecting to transcend the situation immediately.

While in some cases you may be able to access the relative calm of a higher perspective, you will still need to deal with the unfolding consequences of the event over time in your reality. Sometimes your reaction is delayed, so be prepared for either your immediate or eventual emotional upset as a result of resistance to what has occurred, i.e., to the condition.

It is the resistance to 'what is' that most needs to be focused on at this stage. Fear, anxiety, worry and pain are all forms of resistance. Ask yourself, "Can I let go of resisting this illness or disturbance? Can I let go even for a moment? How would I feel if I let go of resisting this?"

Most likely, you will have a response such as "I would feel more peaceful and able to focus on other things, even though it's still there." Then try to feel into that imagined sense of peace and stay with it as long as you can. You will notice your thoughts have quieted and your ability to be present has increased.

Ask yourself those three questions when you sense the initial disturbance has started to settle a bit. Trying to remove resistance at the height of discomfort is not likely to meet with success simply because you will find it hard to focus on the questions or to sense within for the answers.

Too many upsetting sensations and thoughts are likely to be bombarding you.

Before things settle enough to focus off the problem for even a moment, just make it your goal to accept yourself as you are in this new state. The more completely you reach acceptance of your emotional state as in — *Oh, this is my reality right now and this is how it feels* — the quicker you will move on to release your resistance to what has happened.

To sum it up, don't make the mistake of pretending to be "higher" than you are. Accept as normal the upsetting feelings at the onset, and then, when you feel able, release resistance to the event and to your feelings about it by asking the three questions. Your reward for making these small efforts is a sense of release from the emotional stress of the issue as well as the increased likelihood of a better outcome.

In the next chapter, we will consider the spiritual truth about gender while also looking more closely at the purpose of gender in the Surface World.

Chapter 4

You Are Not Your Gender

You've probably heard the expression, "You are not your body," which implies that your consciousness exists in a spiritual dimension beyond ordinary reality. Well the same thing can be said for your gender—most certainly, you are not your gender, much less your gender assignment.

Yes, of course it is true, your illusion body has a gender, most likely male or female, which was assigned to you at birth when you first arrived in this world. That gender assignment is based on the appearance of your genitals, but can also be determined by your DNA.

Your DNA is coded with endless information, not unlike a computer program that is designed to deploy over time. In so doing, it eventually drives the behavior of the individual in the direction of finding a sexual partner and reproducing. This extremely powerful program works in service of survival of the species, and everyone must contend with it.

That said, gender is far more than physical appearance, DNA, and survival programming. It is predominantly a head trip fueled by the heavy cultural programming that everyone is subjected to from the moment of birth.

No wonder some resent the demands, expectations, and limitations heaped upon them because of their gender. Both male and female suffer in their own way from the limiting beliefs associated with the rigid role requirements of being a certain gender. These beliefs are so deeply engrained in the culture that many are not even aware of the programming they have been subjected to, how deep it goes, and how mercilessly it is sustained by the institutions of our culture.

But cultural biases and mental brainwashing, which are the purviews of gender indoctrination, are not where truth lies. By truth, we mean the truth of who you really are.

This world is a shadow play of illusions fueled by the mental acceptance of good and evil. Everything in this world that is not of Spirit is created by man from the mental level. The mental level is a false sense of reality wherein happy events alternate with unhappy ad infinitum.

True peace and true life exist in our Spiritual Home, which is our true identity as Infinite Being. The Infinite is One which knows no duality, no good and evil, no darkness and light, and no haves and have-nots. All that the Infinite is you are as an inseparable part of the Infinite.

It may be hard to conceive of yourself as the grand creator of All That Is, but that is the actual truth of your Being. It would serve you to take time every day in private to contemplate how your 'I' is the actual Being of the Whole. By dwelling on this, you will sooner or later start to feel the presence of your Greater Self and have the mystical experience of God as the substance of all form, including your body and all the forms that constitute your life, as well as the ineffable sensation of moving, breathing and having your being within the Infinite Body of God.

No matter what you have been told about God or the angels, about the ascended masters or even 'the devil', there is no gender in spirit. Source, your true self, is genderless. Therefore, you are, in truth, genderless.

What is being genderless but an embracing, melding and merging of all aspects of gender, all its polarities, and all of its creations. At core, you are in a state of Divine Balance, the true condition of an unconditioned Being free of gender polarity, free of polarization in any aspect of existence.

You can never be apart from your true Source and true Self, the one and only Being in

Existence. Therefore, in relaxing into your true condition as an Infinite Being having a human experience in the illusion world, you may now allow yourself to view your body as it is without any need to change, fix or improve anything about it.

Knowing the truth about your spiritual identity, knowing the nature of this illusion, which spews never-ending polarity and duality in all matters including gender, perhaps now you can put your gender issues into perspective. Perhaps now you can allow your body to be what it is and allow your visible gender to be what it is. Perhaps also, you can free your inner self to embrace the unlimited Being that is your true self.

This new awareness is not something that needs to be externalized or announced such that others may see by your actions or by a difference in your appearance that you have changed. It can simply be like a quiet walk in the park; you enjoy a spacious, peaceful feeling within your own self in recognition of your true condition as Eternal Being.

Chapter 5

What is Identity?

Much is being discussed, written and dramatized in the media about gender identity, making it seem as if it were one of the most important issues of our day, not to mention a most serious issue for every person to ponder, debate, struggle with and, hopefully, understand. Surely all those concerned about their gender identity, or who are experimenting with different 'identities,' would confirm how very real and important their identity concerns are.

But what if I were to tell you that there is only one true Identity, which is your identity as

Infinite Being, and that there is no such thing as gender identity? If you were to run with that idea, you would have to conclude that all this sturm and drang, all this cultural focus on gender identity issues, is a smokescreen; a much ado about nothing. You might then ask the next obvious question which we will address later on: Why is it receiving so much attention at this time in our world?

In fact, gender identity *is* nothing. There is no such thing as gender identity in your true self. However, a false sense of self, which may include a false sense of gender identity, can be created, altered and manipulated by both cultural input and by your own thoughts.

Let us begin to explore this idea by considering how identity is formed. When you are born, you arrive as an unconditioned being into a totally conditioned environment. From your first breath you are inducted in every conceivable way into the world of that environment, which includes the unique circumstances you were born into and the myriad conscious and subconscious beliefs associated with that circumstance.

No newborn stands a chance against the barrage of data imprinted upon it from birth onward, primarily through its family, and eventually through everyone and everything it comes in contact with. In the early days, that might include the pediatrician and the babysitter or day care workers, the toys it plays with, the books that are read to it and the cartoons on the TV. Eventually it includes the schools, the Internet, the media, as well as other kids and their families. Ultimately, it includes the whole of society and all of its institutions and practices.

A child begins their life in an oceanic state of consciousness, deeply merged with what is and with no sense of anything separate from self. Even their mother is perceived as an extension of self and the giver of all good things with whom they are completely merged.

From this undifferentiated state, and while subjected from birth to a veritable storm of cultural programming before they can even make sense of it, a developing child eventually begins to fashion an individual sense of self. That self is heavily shaped by their family who gives subtle or not so subtle cues of approval or disapproval for their various expressions of self.

This socially shaped self becomes a familiar internal feeling that the child associates with 'I.' It becomes the basis of its earliest sense of identity. As experiences in the outer world add to its store of data, the child's sense of 'I' is further enhanced.

Ultimately, the child develops a persona that represents a compromise between their true self and the expectations and demands of their culture. That persona is a mash-up of the beliefs, attitudes and perceptual filters derived from their family of origin, the collective unconscious and their own ongoing life experiences, along with some aspects of their true self.

This is what our culture calls identity: a socially approved false self. This false self creates its own false identity that integrates all the cultural tropes of its era, most especially the programming received from family, friends, medicine, education, government, media and religion, and calls it 'me.'

Nothing true or real can come from a false self with its false stories about identity. Instead of being taught the truth, that you are an Infinite Being having a temporary human experience in an illusion world, and instead of understanding your identity as the One, you are taught you are a separate, biological creature, only slightly better than an animal, trapped in a physical reality. You are further encouraged to remain attached to and self-righteous about the belief systems of your family, culture and country rather than to think for yourself.

Please read the next two paragraphs carefully, as they are a key to your freedom.

One aspect of this false self, with its false stories of who you are, is the popular belief in 'gender identity' when there is no such thing. Gender identity presumes that your true self is defined by your genitalia or, more fashionably, by an alternative identity of the day. There is, in truth, only One Self, that of the Creative Consciousness of All That Is. All other ideas about self, and feelings that you identify with your self, are illusions produced by unconscious programming with its countless false beliefs about reality.

So while you are continuing to be heavily programmed for conformity, which is enforced through social media and the mental prison of political correctness, you are simultaneously being led to believe that something which does not even exist—a unique gender identity—or its close cousin—a new gender assignment—is the fast track to personal freedom.

The real spiritual journey of all human beings is to outgrow their programming, evolve beyond the limitations of their cultural perspective, shed their false self and restore themselves to their true self.

Once awakened to your true self, the true purpose for your lifetime experience and the gifts that will enable it to unfold become apparent. To believe that this spiritual journey involves experimenting with your gender identity or changing your gender is to make a travesty of your real internal, psychological and spiritual maturational process.

All beings are called to become their true self, an identity which has nothing to do with the design of their body or a false sense of self called 'gender identity.' A mature being, meaning one who has integrated and transcended their cultural programming even in small part, will notice that their inner self has no sense of gender whatsoever, that there never was any such thing, and that what is within your being and everyone's being is The Infinite. And what is the Infinite but the part of you that is Divine, Perfect and Whole, which is your true self and your true identity.

If you buy into the false belief in gender identity and in the need to assert your individuality through this false pathway, you are locking yourself further into the cultural mind control that seeks to keep everyone separated from their true power. True power is not accessed through proclaiming your new gender or experimenting with so-called gender identity. It comes from knowing the truth of your being as Consciousness, The All.

Going straight to truth enables you to transcend in one fell swoop a massive amount of the cultural brainwash that would seek to control you and limit you. But it takes emotional strength to not succumb to the social pressure to believe in the false ideas that possess everyone around you.

Social pressure may even present a reasonable and seemingly spirit-freeing purpose behind its rhetoric, which can be very attractive to young people who are barely beginning their journey from the false self to the true self. But that social pressure can and will mislead you, in fact it can direct you into the quicksand from which you may never escape. For there is only one goal of social pressure and that is conformity, the great destroyer of your full self expression as a unique being in this realm.

As you make the journey to uncover your true self, some will go farther than others, some will go hardly anywhere at all. Ultimately, what awaits the most intrepid traveler is the joy and freedom of becoming a transparency for the highest part of you.

At this point you are likely wondering why there is so much discussion about and focus on this latest hot button issue, i.e., gender identity, among your friends, in characters on television shows and movies, in books and magazines, and in the news. In the next chapter, we will take a look at how gender identity and the transgender agenda has been culturally manufactured and explore some of the reasons why.

Chapter 6

The Social Engineering of Gender Dysphoria

Gender dysphoria refers to depression and other mental health issues associated with feeling at odds with your gender assignment and your bodily appearance.

Someone with gender dysphoria tends to see themself as an outcast or outsider and experiences intense discomfort with having to chronically hide their embarrassing problem from others. This often leads to introversion, isolation and obsessive rumination about their issue.

For those suffering from gender dysphoria it is common to feel self-consciousness and discomfort over how you are perceived and treated by others in public, as well as a sense of shame or embarrassment about your body because it does not conform to the body you inwardly feel you should have.

Gender dysphoria is further compounded by the feeling that the person has a big secret and can't be themself or reveal this problem to anyone because they do not expect anyone to understand how they feel.

All of these chronic concerns result in almost constant awareness of and a virtual obsession with gender identity. It may include imagining and wishing they were not their assigned gender, seeking out others who are in conflict like themselves, and experimenting with different gender identities.

While accurate statistics are hard to come by, historically, gender identity issues have appeared in a very tiny percentage of the total population. People with gender dysphoria, including those who are considering gender reassignment, have been estimated to represent only 0.3% of the population, meaning three tenths of one percent of the total US population, i.e., less than one in 300.

That number is really quite small and, to put it in context, is less than the estimated number of people in the US suffering at any given time from one of the following illnesses: Parkinson's Disease, Crohn's Disease or Lupus Disease. How often are they or their issues featured in movies or on television, much less gracing the covers of magazines? Yet have you noticed the massive proliferation of top media coverage by leading news, film and network television of transgender people and the issue of transgender and gender identity?

Perhaps you have also heard or read about new laws and the formation of new departments across schools, medical institutions, mental health facilities, and within the government itself in Canada, Europe and the US, designed to serve the transgender or gender identity afflicted, as if we were preparing for a massive influx of refugees from a war-torn country?

Have you further observed the intense in-crease in social media interest about whether certain male or female TV and movie stars are actually transgender, including those seemingly pregnant? More pointedly, have you noticed how many supposedly male and female actors on television, and to an extent in the movies, look odd, as if they are secretly transgender or are being surgically enhanced with plastic surgery to appear that way?

The all too common suggestion of transgender is most apparent with actors identi-fied as female and who are playing a female role. Many of those actors, far more than would ever occur in the natural order of things, seem to be transgender men! Have you noticed that specula-tion about the real gender of celebrities is not limited to movie stars, but also extends to politi-cians and their husbands or wives, sports heroes, musicians — to essentially all people in the public eye?

Have you wondered why images of openly transgender models are gracing the covers of the biggest magazines in America, including "Time," "Vanity Fair," and "Vogue?" Has it struck you as odd that more openly transgender, transsexual and gender non-binary characters have either leading or supporting roles in some of the most popular shows on television?

Have you ever been curious about why the overwhelming majority of the top male movie stars of all time have taken movie or television roles where they dress in drag and play a female? The names here are too numerous to mention them all, but I will cite a few: Tom Hanks, Robert De Niro, Will Ferrell, Dustin Hoffman, Tom Cruise, Jack Lemmon, Tony Curtis, Robin Williams, Johnny Depp, Nathan Lane, William Dafoe, John Travolta and Adam Sandler. A smaller number of female stars have also dressed in drag and played a male, including Glenn Close, Cate Blanchett, Angelina Jolie, Cameron Diaz and Gwyneth Paltrow.

Is this all just a coincidence, perhaps totally unrelated facts, or maybe a passing trend, not to mention a possible conspiracy theory created by nutcases? Or, could it be that the ascent of the transgender and gender identity issue into public awareness is a deliberately created phenomenon with a social engineering purpose that has been going on for quite some time, and has anything but a humanistic motive.

Let us first consider the origin of any trend that sparks massive public attention. First of all, it is never by accident. It may seem to pop up out of nowhere, like hula hoops or doing the Macarena, but if you were to follow the breadcrumbs backwards, you would find people in positions of power with a plan that is intended to result in their personal benefit. This intended benefit is otherwise known as their motive, usually money and/or increased power. Implementing the plan requires access to a variety of means of disseminating the trend/idea throughout the public arena. This is known as social engineering.

Social engineering is a method of cultural mind control of the masses. In the modern day, it invariably involves the media, where a belief is implanted in the culture and allowed to slowly build and proliferate through multiple media-controlled sources and/or publicized events until it finally goes viral and triggers an automatic pattern of behavior in individuals. The purpose of the social engineering is to ensure an outcome that is ultimately for the benefit of those designing the social engineering experiment.

The public does not realize their behavior has been deliberately shaped and controlled by social engineering, and are likely to feel as if the ideas, beliefs and behaviors that have been gradually installed through repetition and other techniques of mind control are their very own. It feels to them completely natural, as if it has always been there, as if nothing could be more true, real or important than, for example, this gender identity issue arising within themselves and their friends

On the positive side, a social engineering technique can be used to implant helpful ideas that benefit the public, such as not drinking and driving, wearing seatbelts, eating healthy foods, etc. However, this same technique is most often used to implant limiting thought patterns in the culture for the purpose of shaping behavior in a way that serves the interests of the controllers.

Furthermore, to more easily gain in popularity, the control agenda is often portrayed as having a positive or righteous purpose. But like a highly infectious virus that has been deliberately released into society, it has nothing to do with the good of the citizens. If the engineering is successful, then once it has caught on, the public will accept it as normal and effectively monitor their own.

That is the origin of political correctness. Form certain beliefs in the mind of the public. Have the public heavily programmed to avoid certain words or actions that contradict those beliefs, have them programmed to the point of automatically stiffening at the sound of those words or the sight of those acts, indicating that those words or acts have been successfully made into hot buttons. Finally, have them overreact to the sight or sound of those words or acts with harsh judgment and criticism of the source along with behavior intended to stop the source from doing it again.

Hitler used this technique in Germany in the 1930's and 40's with his famous Hitler Youth. These were children and teens programmed to have supreme loyalty to the Fatherland rather than to their friends, parents or teachers. This meant that they were expected to report anyone who expressed ideas or actions that contradicted the policies of the State, and those kids regularly turned people in, including their own parents.

A modern example of social engineering is the hijab/burka dress code as applied to women in Iran. Women who violate the dress code, even just by exposing a tiny bit of hair, might be reported to the 'clothing police' by a neighbor or passerby. The clothing police circulate town to spot these 'non-conforming women.'

Even if it is just her first offense, the woman might be beaten and/or arrested. If she's lucky and can get someone to come down to the station to 'vouch for her,' she may be let off with just severe chastising and made to promise to never violate the dress code again upon threat of being brought in for a whipping.

In the exact same way that Hitler controlled Germany's youth and Iran controls its women, the controlling forces of our society have socially engineered your conflict about your gender and gender identity. The question is, why? Who benefits from having young people turn upon themselves with confusion and dismay about their gender?

The best way to understand this is to look at the consequences of your excessive focus on, ambivalence about or dysphoria regarding your gender. By taking a close look at the consequences of inducing a culture-wide obsession with gender and gender identity, we can deconstruct the intent behind it.

In the next chapter we will explore possible reasons why the controllers of our society would socially engineer a sweeping gender identity movement and how you can elude being snared by its destructive net.

Chapter 7

Gender Identity and its Manipulation

We have already explained in earlier chapters that our true self is genderless and that, therefore, there is no such thing as gender identity, much less is there any basis for inner conflict over something that doesn't exist.

That said, the social engineers of our society, as agents of the transgender agenda, have been very successful in convincing the public that gender identity is a real thing, that, in fact, it is the hot button issue of the day, and that many people are eager to switch genders surgically or otherwise engage in experimentation with their gender identity.

This gender identity trend has been deliberately constructed over a long period time, though reaching ignition more recently through compulsive and ever-increasing focus by the media, both blatant and subtle, on gender and sexism issues, politically correct gender language, gender identity, sexual orientation and homosexuality, and cross-dressing, transsexuals and other transgender matters.

The transgender agenda further seeks to place before the masses an almost unfathomable degree of gender dissemblance in order to subconsciously reconstruct our perceptions of what is male and female. It includes attempting to pass off as female numerous celebrities in film, television, music, sports and politics who, with a bit of study, actually appear to be men in drag, some of whom even claim to be pregnant 'in real life' and display fake baby bumps otherwise known to the film industry as pregnancy prosthetics.

How is this pretense even possible, you may ask? The answer is, through alteration of their appearance with make-up, clothing, hair, hormones and surgery. If you research transgender medical treatments and surgeries, you will learn about the many alterations to one's gender appearance that can be made through medical intervention. Furthermore, by engaging in a scientific study of the differences in male and female anatomy, one discovers the anatomical aspects of men and women that cannot be changed by hormones or surgery.

Once you conduct this kind of research, it eventually becomes obvious that a large number of people receiving intense media exposure across all fields, though pretending to be either female *or* male, may be hiding a reversed gender. The key point here is "people receiving intense media exposure."

Once you grasp the extent of this bizarre situation among the famous and the media darlings, and the variety of transgender tomfoolery that the entertainment, sports and political establishment have been hiding in plain sight for decades, even centuries, shock inevitably sets in. What does it all mean? To experience the curtains pulled back from what has been right in front of your eyes all along, but never before seen for what it is, is to have an awakening that only raises more and more questions.

The controllers of our world, sometimes known as The Illuminati, have long manipulated the masses to not only accept their mind-controlled status as toilers for the rich but to also view it as freedom. In earlier times, they accomplished this by maintaining the masses in survival mode via the feudal system and an unassailable class structure bolstered by religious dogma and rigid gender roles.

The divine right of kings made worship of the monarch akin to worship of God, allowing the king and nobility to utilize the public's false belief in their innate superiority to sustain and justify their hierarchy of power over the poverty-stricken serfs.

Manipulation of the masses by the controllers has been with us as long as civilization has existed. The question is why is gender identity such an important issue for the controllers, and why have they socially engineered a modern day obsession with gender identity and transgender issues. Let us look to the future for our answers because the transgender agenda is part of a long game that we can deconstruct by imagining its ultimate purpose.

Suppose we have a world where the masses have been sold on the need to be microchipped for increased security and efficiency in their daily life, not to mention as a means of paying for resources. These kinds of implants have already been created, with all signs indicating that it is just a matter of time before that agenda is rolled out.

It has even been said that eventually payments will be made by a hand or wrist implant which will replace the credit card and cash, not to mention the smart phone. Those who do not partake would be excluded from engaging in ordinary transactions, thereby losing access to basic resources, which is something most people would never opt for.

It would soon be likely that having accepted one implant, the public would eventually accept more and more technological enhancements, especially if they are purported to increase abilities or provide other supposed advantages. If we look back on how most new social programs are sold to the public, we would see that they are always presented in a light that would make them desirable and necessary while playing down potential problems, not to mention concealing their real purpose. In the case of implants, they would be sold as an essential enhancement while secretly opening the door to increased surveillance and other varieties of control including possible emotional manipulation.

The move to blend humans with artificial intelligence, known as transhumanism, is long believed to be a goal of the Illuminati. Imagine how much more easily humans could be controlled if they are microchipped and otherwise enhanced with implants that could be coded for all kinds of purposes.

Now let us consider that control of the human population best begins at birth or even earlier, and therefore the move to regulate pregnancy and to develop embryos and fetuses in laboratories, becomes the norm, eventually replacing traditional pregnancy and birth. To imagine this is only a short stretch beyond current methods of in vitro and surrogacy, not to mention animal experiments with an artificial uterus and the active practice, and proven viability, of animal cloning.

Furthermore, the female gender would soon be rendered obsolete other than for securing eggs for laboratory breeding programs. However, with the advent of human cloning, females would not even be needed at all because creating a new person only requires one cell with the host DNA.

The resulting human clone would have the same gender as the host, and, in this brave new world, would be predominantly male or, per-haps, some unique designer blend of male and female DNA. Why do we say that? By observing the appearance of famous actors and actresses and other celebrities, we would note that the controllers have a bias toward the male, either the feminized male or the male pretending to be female, as revealed in Hollywood's obsession with male actors in drag, with using numerous transgender performers, a few openly but most secretly, as well as obsessively promoting an aesthetic of female beauty that is far closer to the male body type than to the normal female.

A book of its own could be written on how women are programmed from birth to hate their bodies and strive for a body type that has nothing to do with being female. We refer here to the tall, lean with no body fat, no waist, no hips, small or artificially enhanced breasts, large, angular jaw, high cheekbones, wide shoulders, large clavicle, bony chest, long arms, large hands, male body type which is characteristic of most supposedly female models and many supposedly female movie stars, all of whom receive accolades as the most beautiful 'women' in the world.

When viewed without filters, the agenda becomes clear: many of the most beautiful women in the world actually have the appearance of, and most likely are, transgender or transvestite men. Women have been programmed by the media, as have men, to ignore this deception and view this bizarre body type as the standard for beautiful womanhood.

And why would this social engineering be taking place? It starts to become obvious that the natural female is despised in favor of the transgender appearance of a masculinized female/feminized male. In this way, women have been systematically and intentionally taught to despise themselves and to aspire to an unnatural body type of masculinized femininity as their ideal.

Heterosexual men have also been taught to value this 'female' body type as the ultimate in beauty, and in this way are being deliberately programmed to desire the unnatural female form of a transgender man. They are further encouraged to feminize their own appearance as well, with clothing styles such as skinny jeans, and the increased popularity of applying cosmetics and removing body hair.

In the next chapter, we will add the final pieces to this puzzle of gender identity manipulation and attempt to determine what the controllers' ultimate intent is.

Chapter 8

The Third Gender

It starts to become clear why the public has been inundated with conditioning to move men and women in the direction of androgyny, gender neutrality and other gender varieties: the original need to control populations through traditional male/female gender roles, which was further sustained by religious leaders and religious dogma, has outgrown its relevance in the new world order, and, therefore, a new form of control is needed. That form means turning the population into robotically enhanced servants of the state where everyone is more or less the same, where same-sex sexuality is the primary sexual orientation, where gender and gender roles have little meaning, and where people are conceived in laboratories and as- signed 'designer' genders.

Wouldn't it help the controllers to prepare for this anti-individuality, mind control agenda by programming generations of people to be in denial of their spiritual power as Infinite Being, thus locking the vast majority into body ID and its concomitant obsessive focus on the material world? This would further involve clever media input to create chronic conflict over body type and/or gender identity, thus keeping people constantly focused on themselves and on their body issues, to the point of being in anguish about their gender assignment at birth.

This could only be accomplished if the mass- es have been programmed to fully identify with their body and accept the belief in a solid, biolog- ical world. Body ID is the enemy of higher consciousness and of the spiritual truth that a free mind discovers, i.e., that you are an Infinite Being in an illusion world.

Body ID is the belief that at core you are nothing but a biological entity whose sole purpose is to survive, seek a mate and reproduce or, alternatively, live a life dominated by your issues with your sexual orientation and/or gender assignment.

Body ID further teaches that the body has a life of its own, meaning it has the ability to 'grow up,' 'get sick,' 'get well,' 'contract a disease,' 'deteriorate with age,' and 'die,' not to mention drive its 'owner' to be in conflict over a nonexistent bugaboo called "gender identity" to the point of possibly choosing to adjust it surgically.

The vast majority of people are programmed for this low vibrational, near animal-level of consciousness, a consciousness that is driven by an addiction to the physical world of the senses. Despite modern day trappings, the masses are still motivated at core by survival of the fittest and the need to find protection in a 'herd.' These survival fears result in the compulsive desire to spread one's seed, reproduce and create a tribe, otherwise known as 'the family.'

Naked animal anxiety about survival further underlies modern social behavior, whether you are hooked to your smart phone, posting pictures on social media, spending 'quality time' with your family, 'trying' to get pregnant, or hanging out with your 'besties.' Furthermore, all concerned can then be expected to wag their heads approvingly at your addictive behavior.

Hence, the modern dictate of political correctness, which is one of the controllers' favorite tools of social control. People are programmed to feel safe in the approving arms of conformity, clutching their families and friends ever-closer, with family and parenthood the golden calf of the modern day, rather than being set free to experience life on their own terms.

Such are the imperatives of those who have been split off from their Higher Self and reduced to a low level of consciousness, programmed by the State to breed like cattle no matter that the world population is supposedly increasing by leaps and bounds, and to take no thought for the excessive abuse of resources on their planetary home.

Creating a family — considered the most normal, commonplace thing, and viewed as the gold standard for a quality life — is actually the province of individuals in a lowered vibration who are driven by body ID. It is not typical of the far smaller number of human beings who are, to varying degrees, identified with Spirit (spirit ID), meaning, who are in more advanced levels of consciousness.

Body ID is something a human being must transcend in order to reach a higher state of consciousness. However, the vast majority of people on this planet are in a low to average state of consciousness fostered by the controllers who have benefited for centuries from the unconscious masses with their bodily obsessions and their primal survival fears fueling the need to pass on their genes to progeny and driving them into family units for 'love' and reproduction.

Finally, to this morass we would add the great bugaboo 'gender identity' and its related transgender issues, all part of the soup of body ID which relegates its possessor to a lower vibration and thereby cuts them off from the higher truth that would set them free.

And now we have it. The ultimate purpose of the transgender agenda — with its designer body types, designer gender identities, and total obsession with the body, its appearance and its attractiveness per transgender standards, along with preparation for eliminating the male and female genders, creating a possible 'third gender,' and merging human with robotic technology — is solely to increase and maintain the disconnect between a human being and their higher spiritual truth as the One, the very Infinite Source of All That Is, so that they can be more completely controlled in the New World Order.

Yes, intense effort, persistence and unwavering intent is required to separate a human from their true self and spiritual source, and this unending effort by the controllers has been in place since the beginning of civilization. By separating the people from their true power, which is the spiritual source within each one—Infinite Being, the Substance of All Form—the overlords control the masses and make them serve the interests of those in power.

As the needs of the overlords change so does their agenda. In our concluding chapter, we will take one more look at the transgender agenda and reveal how you can avoid becoming its victim.

In Conclusion

The Trangenderization of America

We have seen that it serves the powers that be to have a large number of the youth of America socially engineered for gender conflict, gender dysphoria and pan or same-sex sexuality. This is further fueled by the media-induced cultural obsession with celebrities, many of whom appear to be closeted transgender 'idols.'

This is not to say that a few of our youth would not be 'different' anyway, as every culture has its small percentage of those who do not fit the prescribed roles of their tribe. But we are referring here to a deliberately created mass phenomenon designed to cast a much wider net.

How do you deal with the subtle yet all-pervasive behavioral conditioning to be dissatisfied with or in denial of your gender at birth and to believe you are in possession of a 'gender identity' at odds with the constricted role you think you will have to play?

What do you make of the programming that aims to convince you that heterosexuality is a straitjacket and encourages you to experiment with homosexuality whether you want to or not?

Finally, as a female, how do you deal with the never-ending barrage of media images, both online and in magazines, billboards, television and movies, that holds up transgender men masquerading as women, or women made to look like transgender men through liposuction, plastic surgery and make-up, as the world class standard of feminine beauty against which you compare yourself and are being compared by your peers?

Within the social programs that have cropped up to increase public acceptance of divergent sexual orientations and gender identities, in both US and European educational, governmental and medical institutions, are the seeds of a much darker purpose. Some of those aware of the dark agenda have gone so far as to connect the dots to implicate Illuminati practices, programs and symbolism, and offer words like 'satanic,' 'alien reptilian' or 'demonic' to explain what is going on.

It is not within the purview of this book to explore alien, interdimensional or supernatural conspiracy theories. Let us just say that the consequences for our society in promoting a transgender agenda, thus creating a population of gender dysphoric, gender identity-obsessed youth, is to lose the mental health of a nation and render the populace even more vulnerable to manifold forms of mind control.

In our spiritual reality as the Deep Self or Originating Consciousness, we have all-power, which really is no power; for in our true state we are the All and Everything and there is nothing to exercise power over. But from the limitational awareness of the surface world, which has carved a false reality out of opposites—good and evil, light and dark, up and down, male and female—we see only endless distortions of truth.

The mind brought back to its natural state as a conduit for the Higher Awareness of the True Self knows that there is no such thing as gender in spirit, much less is there such thing as gender identity. Because the true self of everyone is the One Infinite Consciousness, there is no personal self either within which to harbor a non-existent gender identity.

Your physical gender is solely an artifact of this world of duality and is part of your temporary lifetime experience. Each person is born into this illusion world with a physical illusion body that contains a gender, and lives out a story that enables that person to gather experiential data for their Higher Self.

That said, it may be that your story involves changing your gender, becoming obsessed with your gender and/or accepting the agonizing belief that you have a gender identity that doesn't match your physical gender. To believe, feel or think anything else may seem impossible. If so, this is the nature of your story during this lifetime; you will and must live it out in whatever way you are called to do so.

For some, however, there is choice and there is a moment when a different path may be taken. This book is written for those who are able to consider the possibility that they have been programmed intensively for a very long time, as has the culture in general, to accept many false beliefs that create false issues, including the current obsession with gender roles and gender identity. In this simple understanding freedom can be found.

Furthermore, when the reason or purpose for something is in question, by looking at its consequences we can reverse engineer its original purpose. Therefore, we may conclude that the consequences or results of a certain type of mind control, despite whatever positive spin it may be given, is the true purpose for the mind control.

As an example, let us say you are being mind-controlled, in the name of gender freedom, to have a gender identity obsession or conflict. Because this programming is like a psychic attack on the most primal level of your being, it is guaranteed to tie you up in knots and cause you untold misery in your daily life. Hence, you may discern the true reason for the mind control: your disturbed mental state. By inducing a disturbed mental state, it makes you more vulnerable to further mind control that supports the long game, which is potentially the elimination of male and female genders as we know it and the instituting of a transhumanist agenda.

When ultimately a large portion of the population is obsessed with their gender issues and their gender identity crises, as opposed to looking outward with dissatisfaction and the will-to-change the stultifying institutions governing them, the controllers will have succeeded in moving you that much closer to their ultimate agenda. They will own you; first through your mind and eventually through the implants and altered DNA they will have placed inside your body.

Now that you know the truth, may it set you free.

For those of you who would like to go deeper into the spiritual ideas presented in this book, please visit Amazon.com and check out my foundational work, "Matrix Man: How to Become Enlightened, Happy & Free In An Illusion World." Among the subjects covered in that book are the true nature of reality, how to live in an illusion world, and how to align with Source consciousness.

Before you go, please make sure to download your bonus report, "How to Deconstruct a Troublesome Situation." It will enable you to strip any personal disturbance or life challenge down to its core and open the way for the best solution.

To get your free gift, just go to https://bit.ly/DeconstructSituation.

Did You Enjoy This Book?

Dear Reader,

Thank you for reading *Transgender America: Spirit, Identity, And The Emergence Of The Third Gender*. I hope you enjoyed it. My purpose in writing this book was to help you and your loved ones understand the transgender agenda and find inner freedom from the growing cultural obsession with gender identity.

If you would like to recommend this book to other readers, please write a brief review on Amazon. It will only take a few minutes, and I would appreciate it very much.

Thanks again, and wishing you the very best!

S. F. Howe

Books by S. F. Howe

MIND · BODY · SPIRIT

HIGHER CONSCIOUSNESS

Matrix Man: How To Become Enlightened, Happy And Free In An Illusion World

The author reveals a new reality paradigm that will liberate you from the limiting beliefs and programs that prevent a joyful and fulfilling life. Available in print and digital editions.

The Top Ten Myths Of Enlightenment: Exposing The Truth About Spiritual Enlightenment That Will Set You Free!

Essential reading for spiritual seekers. What no one else will tell you to help you avoid the pitfalls of the spiritual journey. Available in print and digital editions.

PLANT INTELLIGENCE

Secrets Of The Plant Whisperer: How To Care For, Connect, And Communicate With Your House Plants

A plant whisperer reveals the hidden truth about plants and why relating to them in a conscious way is vital for their health and well-being. Available in print and digital editions.

Your Plant Speaks!: How To Use Your Houseplant As A Therapist

Let your house plant solve your problems! Discover the little known art of receiving life coaching from your favorite indoor plant.
Coming Soon!

PERSONAL GROWTH

Vision Board Success: How To Get Everything You Want With Vision Boards!

A powerful technique for achieving your goals and manifesting your desires. Available in print and digital editions.

Sex Yoga: The 7 Easy Steps To A Mind-Blowing Kundalini Awakening!

A technique for activating the chakras to induce a powerful kundalini experience. Available in print and digital editions.

Morning Routine For Night Owls: How To Supercharge Your Day With A Gentle Yet Powerful Morning Routine!

Morning rituals aren't only for morning people, and they don't have to be rough and tumble or performed at top speed to set up a perfect day. Welcome to the world of the gentle yet powerful wake-up routine for night owls! Available in print and digital editions.

Books by S. F. Howe

CONSCIOUS HEALTH

Transgender America: Spirit, Identity, And The Emergence Of The Third Gender

A higher consciousness perspective on the Transgender Agenda; what it is and why it is being rolled out at breakneck speed to socially engineer a gender dysphoria epidemic. Available in print and digital editions.

When Nothing Else Works: How To Cure Your Lower Back Pain Fast!

The simple method that no doctor will ever tell you about. Requires no drugs, no surgery, and no special equipment. Available in print and digital editions.

About the Author

S. F. Howe is a psychologist, author and spiritual teacher. Howe began teaching psychology at the university level while a doctoral candidate in clinical psychology, and went on to work in hospitals and clinics for more than 25 years as a psychotherapist, staff psychologist, clinical program consultant and director of chemical dependency and psychiatric programs.

In the midst of graduate studies, a profound spiritual awakening led to a complete reevaluation of the author's life path. Thus began a spiritual journey along the road less traveled, extending far beyond clinical psychology, conventional reality paradigms and both traditional religion and new age spirituality.

While engaged in a unique, ongoing process of discovery, the author enjoys sharing with others an ever-expanding understanding of the true nature of reality. This has resulted in

Howe's noted books and teachings on the subjects of higher consciousness, conscious health, personal growth and plant intelligence.

Howe's primary intention is to bring an end to suffering by guiding others on a well-worn path to truth and expanded awareness. Many of those who have experienced Howe's input and presence report emotional and physical healing, life-changing realizations and dramatic personal transformation.

S. F. Howe may be contacted for speaking and teaching engagements. Please direct all inquiries to info@diamondstarpress.com.

Free Gift

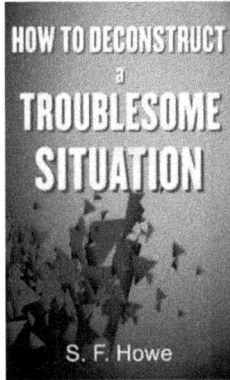

As my thanks to you for reading *Transgender America: Spirit, Identity, And The Emergence Of The Third Gender,* I would like you to have the bonus report, "How to Deconstruct a Troublesome Situation." Inside this report is a powerful technique that will help you strip any problem down to its core and give you the objectivity needed to find the best solution.

To download your free gift, just go to https://bit.ly/DeconstructSituation.